MW00465246

Conversations

on

My Grandmother Asked Me to Tell You She's Sorry

Fredrik Backman

By dailyBooks

FREE Download: Get the Hottest Books!

*Get Your Free Books with **Any Purchase** of* Conversation Starters!

Every purchase comes with a FREE download of the hottest titles!

Add spice to any conversation
Never run out of things to say
Spend time with those you love

Read it for FREE on any smartphone, tablet, Kindle, PC or Mac.

No purchase necessary - licensed for personal enjoyment only.

Get it Now

or Click Here.

Scan Your Phone

Tips for Using dailyBooks Conversation Starters:

EVERY GOOD BOOK CONTAINS A WORLD FAR DEEPER THAN the surface of its pages. The characters and their world come alive through the words on the pages, yet the characters and its world still live on. Questions herein are designed to bring us beneath the surface of the page and invite us into the world that lives on. These questions can be used to:

- Foster a deeper understanding of the book
- Promote an atmosphere of discussion for groups
- Assist in the study of the book, either individually or corporately
- Explore unseen realms of the book as never seen before

About Us:

THROUGH YEARS OF EXPERIENCE AND FIELD EXPERTISE, from newspaper featured book clubs to local library chapters, *dailyBooks* can bring your book discussion to life. Host your book party as we discuss some of today's most widely read books.

Table of Contents

Introducing *My Grandmother Asked Me to Tell You She's Sorry*

MY GRANDMOTHER ASKED ME TO TELL YOU SHE'S SORRY IS a simple and heartwarming story about a young girl called Elsa. Elsa is a special needs child and is much smarter than the average child. Because of this, she is shunned by most adults and is bullied by other children. Her grandmother is her only friend, and they love each other very much. But Granny has terminal cancer and a while before Elsa's eighth birthday, she dies. This leaves Elsa devastated and angry, so much so that she at first is totally disinclined to follow up on the mission her grandmother has entrusted to her.

When Elsa's parents divorced, Elsa had trouble sleeping and was generally very upset with the situation. At this time, Granny invented The Land of Almost Awake, in which there were six kingdoms, each known for their specific characteristics. Elsa spent all her time in this land of make-believe. Through these fairy tales, Granny tried to teach Elsa things about real life. It was only after Granny's death that Elsa realizes that the fairy tales meant much more than she had at first thought.

Granny left Elsa letters to be delivered to several people, most of them living in the "house," which was a building divided into several flats. Different people and families lived in these flats, and each of them had some kind of problem. Their behavior was often atrocious, and they did not ever get together as a housing society. Behind the obvious, lay a history that Elsa sets out to discover through her grandmother's mission. She discovers the sad stories of the people in the building and shows her empathy. She realizes that Granny had helped them all over the years, and they, in turn, help Elsa. Gradually, there is healing for everyone.

This book is different because of the way the fairy tales effortlessly weave into the real life stories of the inhabitants of the house. When Elsa tries to unravel the secret histories of the people with whom she is surrounded, she also unravels the deeper and hidden meanings of the fairy tales her grandmother told her.

Introducing the Author

FREDRIK BACKMAN IS A SWEDISH AUTHOR WHOSE FIRST book, *A Man Called Ove*, became a phenomenal success, both in Sweden and around the world. Backman became a household name, and he was even nominated Sweden's most successful author in 2013, the year the book was published.

Backman grew up in Helsingborg, a scenic coastal city to the north of the country. He had ambitions of becoming a journalist but ended up studying religion instead. At some point, he lost interest in it and resorted to sending his writing to magazines and publications while driving a truck to make ends meet. He began to receive small writing assignments and eventually got a regular column at *Xtra*. He has also written for the *Moore Magazine* and *Metro*. However, it was when he started a blog that he got his first major breakthrough as an author. Backman is an extremely popular blogger who has blogged about his wedding preparations and his experiences with fatherhood.

He kept a personal blog and recorded various experiences in it and shared some of his writing as well. One piece of writing that became very popular with his readers was a character, which ultimately developed into Ove in the book *A Man Called Ove*. His readers encouraged him to weave the character into a book, and this was when Backman started to write seriously. He has since released two more books, both of which have done well. His first and most famous book is also going to be made into a movie. It has also been developed into a play and is popular in Stockholm.

He is working on several new projects but doesn't have any writing routine as such. He writes whenever he has the time and enjoys it. Backman is married and lives with his wife and children, juggling his writing career with being a stay-at-home dad.

Discussion Questions

question 1

The monster was a refugee from a war-torn country. It is never specified which country he was from, but there are clues. The names of the fantasy kingdoms mean something more concrete to him. Which language do you think the monster spoke, and which country and war were referred to, according to you? Discuss.

question 2

There are many well-defined characters in the book that act as a background to Elsa's story. Which one of these is your favorite, and why?

question 3

Granny told Elsa a lot of fairy tales over the years, and some of them had become canon for this make-believe land. Which one is your favorite story, and why?

. . . .

question 4

Granny goes around behaving irresponsibly and picking fights with people. Do you think she is a good person to take charge of a child, no matter how much she loved the child? Why or why not?

. . . .

. . . .

question 5

Mum was angry with Granny because she felt abandoned during her childhood. Do you think Mum felt the same anger against her father? Would the presence of her father have helped her handle the situation better? Discuss.

. . . .

. . . .

question 6

One of the themes of this book is the power of stories. Do you think fairy tales are important for children? Why or why not? What other importance could fairy tales have?

. . . .

question 7

Elsa often quotes the Harry Potter series in different contexts. Why do you think she is so enamored of the books? What do you think kids can learn from the Harry Potter series?

. . . .

question 8

Elsa regularly gets bullied at school. What can we do as a society to stop the bullying of and by children? Do you think your community has decent anti-bullying practices in place?

question 9

This book talks about how Elsa is different from all the other students in her school. Do you think precocious and over-smart kids make adults uncomfortable? Why or why not? How do you think adults generally react to such children? How do you think adults should behave with such children?

. . . .

question 10

Elsa was terrified and couldn't sleep when her parents divorced. Divorce generally affects children in a negative way. How do you think people can negate the impact of their divorce on their children? Do you think it would be possible to educate them on this aspect during a stressful time? Discuss.

question 11

Elsa was born on the same day of the tsunami when millions of people lost their lives, homes, and occupations. This was the last mission that Granny attended after which she left her job to take care of Elsa. Why do you think Granny quit her job at this stage?

question 12

One of the characters in the book was the "boy with the syndrome." What syndrome do you think he has? Do you recognize the symptoms of his problem? How do you think the people around him should support him?

· ·

question 13

Elsa hated George at times just because everyone liked him. Why
do you think this was so? Do you think George did something to
make Elsa hate him? What are your thoughts on Elsa's
relationship with George?

· ·

question 14

Sam was abusive to his wife and son. Why do you think the mother did not leave to save herself and her son? What precautions could be taken to prevent such men from having power over those who are unable to care for themselves?

question 15

Elsa's conversation with the policewoman showed that the police are there for the protection of everyone. She claims that her job is to protect both the innocents and the culprits. Do you agree? Why would this be a better approach than dismissing those who commit crimes as less than human?

question 16

Publisher's Weekly considers that Elsa's narrative did not succeed as well as Backman's previous work. Do you agree? What do you think is lacking in *My Grandmother Asked Me to Tell You She's Sorry* as compared to *A Man Called Ove*?

question 17

Kirkus Reviews compares Backman with popular authors like Roald Dahl and Neil Gaiman. What do you think is similar about the work of these three authors?

. . . .

question 18

Kelly Garbato in her blog *Vegan Daemon* says that the writing
was initially too cutesy, but she quickly grew into it. What are
your thoughts about the writing technique in the book? How do
you think it could have been made better?

. . . .

. . . .

question 19

The Courier-Tribune posted a review of this book by Terri Schlichenmeyer that claimed that Elsa had to grow up fast, but this was mercifully aborted by the posthumous wishes of her grandmother. Do you agree? By sending Elsa on the kind of mission she does and willing the house to her, does Granny indicate a contribution to her growing up quickly or delaying the same?

. . . .

. . . .

question 20

BookNAround blog posted a review saying that Elsa was too precocious and therefore hard to believe as a 7-year-old. Do you agree? Why or why not? How would you have preferred Elsa to be portrayed?

. . . .

. . . .

question 21

In the review in the *BookNAround* blog, the reviewer claims that the plot was dominated by the long-running fairy tale. Do you agree? Do you think the fairy tale added to the book or detracted from it? How would this story have played out without the fairy tale?

. . . .

. . . .

question 22

In the blog, *Dog-Eared & Dog-Tagged*, the reviewer claims that
Granny was in the business of saving people, and that only Elsa
can complete the work. Do you think a seven-year-old child can
do this kind of work even if she is smart? Who, in your opinion,
would be best suited to take on Granny's mantle, and why?

. . . .

. . . .

question 23

In the blog *Book Pleasures*, the reviewer says that the star of the book is Backman's prose. He balances whimsical word choices with literary brilliance and takes readers along for a magical journey. Do you agree? Why or why not? Which, according to you, is the best part of the book?

. . . .

question 24

Backman wrote two books other than this one, *A Man Called Ove* and *Britt-Marie Was Here*. According to the review in *Bymarlida* blog, this book is a little different than the other two. What do you think makes this book different from the other work of the author?

question 25

In the blog *Jen's Book Thoughts*, the reviewer claims that Elsa's coping mechanisms for life are humorous, yet also charming and authentic. What do you think of Elsa's coping mechanisms? Do you think they work for a seven-year-old?

question 26

A Man Called Ove was Backman's first book and was a huge hit. His publishers wanted him to write Ove 2. Do you think it's difficult to match the runaway success of the first book for such authors in general? How could they deal with this pressure?

question 27

Fredrick Backman was a blogger and journalist first before he became an author. How do you think having a background in writing helps writers develop better plots and characters?

question 28

Backman is a stay-at-home dad who feels his time is taken up with his kids, so he can't manage to find a routine for his writing. Do you think this kind of lifestyle facilitates your writing or makes it more difficult? Why?

· ·

question 29

Backman's first book is going to be made into a movie though he doesn't have much of a say in the script. As an author, would you want to take this risk of having someone else adapt your work in a way completely different from what you have envisaged?

question 30

Backman agrees that there is an autobiographical element to every book he writes. Which part of *My Grandmother Asked Me to Tell You She's Sorry* do you think is influenced by his real life?

question 31

Granny created a fairy tale land for Elsa that had six kingdoms: Miamas, Mirevas, Mipolaris, Mimovas, Miaudacas, and Mibatalos. Each of these lands has their own specific functions and characteristics. Elsa spent most of her time in Miamas. Which one would you prefer to inhabit if you were Elsa, and why?

. . . .

question 32

Granny made a difficult choice when she decided to go to help
people who needed her though she had to leave her child alone at
home. If you were Granny, what choice would you have made
under these circumstances, and why?

. . . .

. . . .

question 33

Granny was an irresponsible and immature woman when it came to many things. She could even be considered completely crazy. If you were Mum, would you have entrusted your daughter to her? Why or why not?

. . . .

question 34

Britt-Marie had two brothers in love with her—Alf and Kent. She had a relationship with Alf, but they split up when she discovered he was having an affair. She finally ended up marrying Kent. If you were Britt-Marie, which brother would you have preferred to marry, and why?

question 35

Elsa claims that everyone has their own superpowers. What do you think is your superpower, and why?

· ·

question 36

Granny left the house to Elsa in her will since she felt that Elsa would take care of the responsibilities that went with it better than anyone else. If you were in Granny's place, to whom would you have left the house, and why?

· ·

question 37

Elsa considers comic books as quality literature. What kind of books did you consider as quality literature when you were a child, and why?

question 38

Maud and Lennart chose to help their grandson and daughter in law rather than their son, though when he was in prison, they went to see him regularly to try and help him. If you were Maud or Lennart, how would you have dealt with a son like Sam?

Quiz Questions

. . . .

question 39

Granny was a _____ by profession.

. . . .

question 40

There were _____ kingdoms in the Land of Almost Awake.

question 41

_____ is the place from where most fairy tales came.

question 42

Alf was in love with _____.

question 43

Granny left _____ to Elsa in her will.

question 44

True or false: Monster was actually a refugee.

question 45

True or false: Kent was faithful to Britt-Marie.

question 46

My Grandmother Asked Me to Tell You She's Sorry was Backman's _____ book.

question 47

Backman's first choice of a career was _____.

question 48

_____ gave rise to Backman's first book.

question 49

True or false: Backman has a strict work routine.

· ·

question 50

Backman is from _____.

· ·

Quiz Answers

1. doctor
2. six.
3. Miamas
4. Britt-Marie
5. the house
6. True
7. False;
8. second
9. journalism
10. blogging
11. False; Backman is a stay-at-home dad and snatches time from his hectic life to write. He prefers it this way.
12. Helsingborg

THE END

Want to promote your book group? Register here.

PLEASE LEAVE US A FEEDBACK.

THANK YOU!